Oprah Winfrey

An Unauthorized Biography

Gini Holland

Heinemann
LIBRARY

www.heinemann.co.uk

Visit our website to find out more information about **Heinemann Library** books.

To order:

 Phone 44 (0) 1865 888066

 Send a fax to 44 (0) 1865 314091

Visit the Heinemann Bookshop at www.heinemann.co.uk to browse our catalogue and order online.

First published in Great Britain by Heinemann Library, Halley Court, Jordan Hill, Oxford OX2 8EJ, a division of Reed Educational and Professional Publishing Ltd.
Heinemann is a registered trademark of Reed Educational & Professional Publishing Limited.

OXFORD MELBOURNE AUCKLAND JOHANNESBURG BLANTYRE GABORONE IBADAN PORTSMOUTH NH (USA) CHICAGO

Produced for Heinemann Library by Discovery Books Limited
Designed by Ian Winton
Originated by Dot Gradations
Printed and bound in Hong Kong/China

ISBN 0431 08656 7 (paperback)   ISBN 0431 08648 6 (hardback)
05 04 03 02   05 04 03 02 01
10 9 8 7 6 5 4 3 2 1   10 9 8 7 6 5 4 3 2 1

British Library Cataloguing in Publication Data

Holland, Gini
Oprah Winfrey. – (Heinemann Profiles)
1. Winfrey, Oprah, 1954– – Juvenile literature 2. Women television personalities – United States – Biography – Juvenile literature 3. Television personalities – United States – Biography – Juvenile Literature 4. Talk shows – United States – Biography – Juvenile Literature
I. Title
629.1'3'092

Acknowledgements
The Publishers would like to thank the following for permission to reproduce photographs:
Aquarius pp23, 29, 40; Corbis pp7, 10, 11, 12, 17, 20, 21, 26, 31, 32, 39; Gini Holland pp14, 15; Popperfoto pp9, 33, 35, 37, 51; Rex Features pp5, 28, 30, 42, 45, 47, 48; Topham Picture Point p34.

Cover photograph reproduced with permission of Popperfoto

Every effort has been made to contact copyright holders of any material reproduced in this book. Any omissions will be rectified in subsequent printings if notice is given to the Publisher.

Any words appearing in the text in bold, **like this**, are explained in the Glossary.

Major Sources
Bill Adler, ed, *The Uncommon Wisdom of Oprah Winfrey: a portrait in her own words*. New York: Carol Publishing Group, 1997.
Nellie Bly, *Oprah! Up Close and Down Home*. New York: Kensington Publishing Company, 1993.
George Mair, *Oprah Winfrey: The Real Story*. Secaucus, New York: Carol Publishing Group, 1994.
Robert Waldron, *Oprah!* New York: St. Martin's Press, 1987.

CONTENTS

WHO IS OPRAH WINFREY?

There are many talk-show hosts on American television, but there is only one Oprah. Her unique style is copied by many, from interviewers to politicians. But none has been able to match either her popularity or her income. Her *Oprah Winfrey Show* is broadcast to 132 countries worldwide. Her combined talents and business sense will soon make Oprah the United States' first African-American billionaire. Her show has received over thirty **Emmys** and numerous other awards for achievement.

Some blame Oprah for turning daytime television into a string of shows about freaks and terrible relationships. In spite of this charge, she is one of her country's most beloved celebrities – and one of its

Being famous

Fame is a major factor in Oprah's daily life, but it took her by surprise at first. She once said: 'I was walking down the street the other day, and a woman bus driver pulled her bus over, jumped off it, and ran down the street to shake my hand. The bus was full, and this was five o'clock traffic, but the passengers loved it. Everyone was clapping, and I said to myself, "This is something. I must be a somebody!"'

most influential people. In the USA, over twenty million viewers a week watch her show. She has an Internet website packed with topics of interest for her audience. Her new magazine, *O*, puts her point of view on the news stands. Harpo, her **production company**, produces movies for television and cinema. Whether these shows star Oprah herself or other actors, they are stamped with her values and ideas.

In 1988, Oprah received the People's Choice Award and the International Radio and Television Society's award as Broadcaster of the Year.

MOST TRUSTED

What is her secret to success? She is possibly the most trusted woman in America. Her fans trust her to entertain, inspire, educate and understand. They trust her to accept them just as they are, even when she challenges them to be better. At the same time, to many, Oprah Winfrey feels like a television version of their favourite next-door neighbour. In fact, most of her fans are not in awe of her – they just want to invite her round for coffee.

Early Years in Changing Times

Oprah Winfrey was born on 29 January 1954 to unmarried teenage parents, in Kosciusko, Mississippi, one of the poorest areas of the USA. Her biblical name Orpah was misspelt on her birth certificate by the midwife, making her Oprah. No one ever corrected the mistake. When she was still a baby, her mother, Vernita Lee, left Oprah to be raised by her maternal grandparents.

At her grandparents' farm, Oprah was poor, and lonely. 'The nearest neighbour was a blind man up the road. There weren't other kids ... no playmates, no toys except for the one **corncob doll**. I played with the animals and made speeches to the cows.'

Speaking from experience

Oprah lived in terror of her grandfather, who tried to shoo her away with his cane. Her grandmother beat Oprah when she misbehaved. She told Oprah that she was doing it for her own good, because she loved her. 'I still don't think that was love,' says Oprah now, and she has often spoken out on her shows against child abuse, believing that it is partly to blame for many of society's problems today, because of the message of violence and lack of understanding it sends to young people.

'Oprah's law'

In 1991 Oprah testified before the US Senate on behalf of the National Child Protection Act that she herself had initiated. This resulted in a national law, that requires that all convicted child abusers be listed on a national database. Known to many as the 'Oprah bill', or 'Oprah's law', it was signed into law in her presence by President Clinton on 20 December 1993.

Oprah Winfrey speaking at the inauguration of President Clinton, 17 January 1993. In that same year she witnessed President Clinton signing into law the 'Oprah bill' against child abuse.

LOVE OF LEARNING

Oprah's grandmother taught her to read by the time she was three. When Oprah started **kindergarten** at the age of five – the time when most children start being taught to read in the USA – she was bored. Fortunately, Oprah was good at speaking up for herself, even then. She wrote her teacher a note: 'Dear Miss New. I don't think I belong here.' Impressed with Oprah's skills, Miss New moved her up to first **grade** – with the six year olds – right away.

'Reading gave me hope. For me it was the open door.'
Oprah Winfrey, 1997

Bigger changes lay ahead. Around 1960, Oprah was moved north to Milwaukee, Wisconsin, to live with her mother. Oprah had to get used to living in a city instead of the country, and to living with a parent she barely knew. She did not feel at home there, or even very welcome. 'I felt like I was an outcast. I don't know why mother ever decided she wanted me. She wasn't equipped to take care of me. I was just an extra burden to her.' Oprah's half-sister, Patricia, had lighter skin, which Oprah thought made her prettier. So Oprah decided that she would take comfort in being the cleverer of the two.

At the end of first grade Oprah moved south again, this time to Nashville, Tennessee, to live briefly with her father, Vernon Winfrey. Once again, teachers

Milwaukee, Wisconsin, in the 1960s, about the time when Oprah was moved there to live with her mother, whom she barely knew.

recognized her ability and moved her up, this time to third grade. Then she returned to live with her mother in Milwaukee. Despite being shuffled between parents, she did well in school and learnt how to work hard to get ahead. 'I felt it happen in the fourth grade. Something came over me. I turned in a book report early and it got such a good response, I thought, "I'm gonna do that again."'

LEARNING DIFFERENT RULES

Moving between two parents showed her the difference that parents' expectations and limits can make. 'Growing up, I acted differently when being raised by my mother than being raised by my father. [With her] I would break **curfew**. I'd stay out. I'd run the streets. Because I knew I could get away with it … On the other hand, my father didn't even have to say it. You just knew.…'

SEGREGATION AND POVERTY

In the 1950s, being African-American meant you could be legally **segregated** from white society. You could not attend white-only schools. African-American-only schools, in both the north and the south, had less money for teachers, books, buildings, and even heating, than white schools did. African-Americans in the United States are still in a minority (currently 13 per cent), compared to whites. However, they now have civil rights – legal rights equal to those in the white majority.

In the north, racist landlords prevented African-Americans from living in good neighbourhoods. Racial Discrimination barred them from well-paid jobs. Oprah Winfrey, like most African-Americans then, lived in poverty. When she shared a bedroom with her half-brother and sister in Milwaukee, she

During much of Oprah's early childhood, segregation laws barred African-Americans from attending white-only schools. These people are demonstrating against integration.

remembers: 'We were so poor we couldn't afford a dog or cat, so I made pets out of two cockroaches.… You wanted pets, all you had to do was go in the kitchen at night and turn on the lights. You could find a whole family of them. So I would name them and put them in a jar and feed them.… I called them things like Melinda and Sandy.'

Blacks lack political power

Hardest of all, in most of the rural south, African-American adults were denied the vote until the **civil rights movement** became active in the '60s.

They had no political power and no representation. There were no African-American **mayors**, **sheriffs** or **senators** to look out for their interests.

African-American workers were usually the 'last hired, first fired'. They were almost always paid less than white workers. With no power and little money or education, African-American families were not only at the bottom of society: they were supposed to stay there.

THE BIRTH OF CIVIL RIGHTS

1954, the year Oprah was born, marked the first time that the US Supreme Court ruled that **segregation** was not legal. The case was *Brown* v *The Board of Education*. The parents of a seven-year-old girl, Linda Brown, successfully sued the school board in Topeka, Kansas to allow their daughter to attend her local, white-only school. This case ended legal school segregation in the United States.

The following year, on 1 December 1955, an African-American woman named Rosa Louise Parks

Rosa Parks, whose protest against bus segregation paved the way for the progress in African-American civil rights.

refused to give up her bus seat to a white man in Montgomery, Alabama. She was arrested and fined for violating segregation laws.

African-Americans in Montgomery sought the help of the civil rights leader Dr Martin Luther King Jr, and they organized a year-long boycott of the buses. Eventually, the Supreme Court declared bus segregation laws illegal. By the end of 1955, schools and public transport were fully open to African-Americans for the first time. Rosa Parks has been called 'the mother of the **civil rights movement**' because her simple act of courage led to one of the first successes of non-violent protest for civil rights.

THE AIM OF CIVIL RIGHTS

In the late 1950s and throughout the 1960s, the civil rights movement worked hard to change the country from segregation to **integration**. The goal was to have people of all races and religions living in harmony, sharing equal civil rights and equal opportunities.

But there was a price to pay for changing from '**Coloured**' or 'Negro' to 'Black and Beautiful' at the height of the civil rights movement. Oprah herself was to learn that lesson when integration provided her with a new educational opportunity.

INTEGRATING TWO WORLDS

Moving backwards and forwards between relatives, Oprah learnt to make the best of changing rules and adult expectations. But perhaps her biggest challenge came in high school.

FREED FROM SEGREGATION

One of Oprah's teachers, Eugene A Abrams, made it happen. Around 1966, Oprah was enrolled at Lincoln High School in Milwaukee, 99 per cent of whose students were African-American. The classes were overcrowded and the building was run down. Most students were from poor, uneducated families. It was hard to work well in such an environment.

One day Mr Abrams saw Oprah reading in the cafeteria during lunch. This was not the way most of his students behaved! Realizing what a serious student Oprah was, Abrams helped her get a scholarship to Nicolet, an all-white, academically strong high school in the wealthy **suburb** of Fox Point.

Lincoln High School, Milwaukee, where Oprah went to school until 1967. Conditions in inner-city schools at that time made learning difficult.

COOL TO BE BLACK

Thanks to the growing **civil rights movement**, **integration** was becoming the 'right thing' to do. Oprah remembers, 'It was the first time that I was exposed to the fact that I was not like all the other kids. In 1968 it was real hip to know a black person, so I was very popular.' This kind of false popularity made her feel uneasy. 'The kids would all bring me back to their houses, bring out their maid from the back, and say, "Oprah, do you know Mabel?" They figured all blacks knew each other. It was real strange and real tough.'

RICH FRIENDS, POOR FAMILY

The thirty-kilometre bus ride home from Fox Point to the inner city was like commuting between different planets: 'The life that I saw those children lead was so totally different than what I went home to. I wanted my mother to be like their mothers... But her way of showing love to me was getting out and going to work every day, putting clothes on my back, and having food on the table. At that time I didn't understand it.'

OPRAH CHANGES COURSE

The stress of living in two worlds, one rich, one poor, was often too much for Oprah, on top of which there were other problems with family and friends. She began to disobey her mother and get into trouble. Eventually, Oprah tried to steal $200 from her and run away. Desperate, Vernita threatened to put Oprah in a home for troubled teenagers. But when the home couldn't take her immediately, Vernita called Oprah's father, who fetched her back to live with him and his wife in Nashville.

SAVED BY HER FATHER

Her father was strict, but Oprah is grateful: 'When my father took me, it changed the course of my life. He saved me. He simply knew what he wanted and expected. He would take nothing less.'

'My father turned my life around by making me see that being your best was the best you could be. His love of learning showed me the way... I have a great father who used to tell me, "listen, girl, if I tell you a mosquito can pull a wagon, don't ask me no questions. Just hitch him up."'

Oprah Winfrey, 1997

Vernon Winfrey set a firm dress code for Oprah. Halter tops and tight, short skirts were forbidden. He wanted her to look and behave like a proper young lady. He demanded excellence from her in school work as well.

A portrait of an early Oprah role model, Sojourner Truth (c 1797–1883). A former slave, she became a travelling preacher.

ROLE MODELS FROM HISTORY

Because Oprah read so much, many of her **role models** came from history. One of the first speeches Oprah memorized remains one of her favourites:

Sojourner Truth's powerful 'Ain't I a Woman?' speech. Sojourner Truth was a slave who, after a long struggle to win her own freedom, spoke at the Women's Rights Convention in Akron, Ohio, in 1851: 'That man over there says that a woman needs to be helped into carriages and lifted over ditches and have the best place everywhere. Nobody ever helps me into carriages or over mud puddles or gives me any best place and ain't I a woman?…'

FIRST SUCCESSES

Under her father's roof, Oprah began to thrive. One of the first African-Americans to attend East Nashville High School, she was voted 'Most Popular Girl', but this time she could cope with, and enjoy, the attention she received. Vernon drove her to speaking competitions all over the state. The experience of public speaking turned out to be very beneficial to her career.

She became an **honours student**, and her hard work began to pay off in both travel and awards. At seventeen, Oprah was invited to President Nixon's

Early tragedy

Instead of becoming one of the world's most famous entertainers and richest women, Oprah could have become a teenage unmarried mother. At the age of fourteen, Oprah gave birth to a baby boy after a pregnancy of only six months. The baby died shortly afterwards. When her half-sister told national magazines about this dark secret, Oprah turned a negative situation into a positive one by discussing it on her show. She has made a point of discussing the problems of teens, the key causes of teen pregnancy, and the tough choices some teens have to make.

White House Conference on Youth in Estes Park, Colorado. She competed for the title of 'Outstanding Teenager of America'. After winning first place in the National Forensic League Tournament in Tennessee, a contest for speakers and debaters, she went on to compete (unsuccessfully) against other winners from around the nation in the final at Stanford University, Palo Alto, California.

A BREAK IN RADIO

In 1971, while still in high school, Oprah's speaking abilities and personality helped her get her first job in broadcasting. Disc jockey John Heidelberg 'discovered' her when she asked him to sponsor her in a charity walk. 'I admired her voice,' he explained later. 'She was articulate.' After persuading her father to allow her to take the job, she began to train and then work after school and weekends at the local radio station, WVOL. She read the news for $100 a week – the beginning of her media career.

Technical tips

○ John Heidelberg taught Oprah the technical parts of her job, how to speak into a
○ microphone without hissing on her s's and puffing on her p's, and to never turn her head
○ away from the microphone when speaking.

COLLEGE AND CROWNS

An African-American beauty contest of the 1970s. Prize money from beauty contests like these helped Oprah pay her college tuition fees. She won on poise and talent.

After high school, Oprah attended college at Tennessee State University, although her developing career would mean that it was many years before she would graduate. Many young people cannot afford the expense of college, but Oprah found a way. She competed in beauty contests, where her talents in acting often made her a winner. Beauty contests helped her pay her tuition fees and polish her stage skills. Best of all, they also brought exciting travel opportunities.

In March 1972, she was crowned Miss Black Nashville, then went on to win Miss Black

Tennessee. 'I won on poise and talent. I was raised to believe that the lighter your skin, the better you were. I wasn't light-skinned, so I decided to be the best and the smartest.' As Miss Black Tennessee, she not only won a scholarship, but received an all-expenses-paid trip to Hollywood for the Miss Black America pageant.

Stars leave their prints and signatures in this Hollywood pavement. Becoming a star was Oprah's childhood dream.

Going to Hollywood and becoming a star was a childhood dream for Oprah. She didn't win the Miss Black America crown, but she touched the names of stars written in the Hollywood pavements. She just knew her name would be there some day, and, to make her dream of acting come true, she made speech and drama her major course of study in college.

BLACK PRIDE, OPRAH-STYLE

Unlike many African-Americans at that time, Oprah did not demonstrate in Black Pride activities. Oprah took a different path to Black Pride: she worked to push past **stereotypes**, to do things that had previously been for 'Whites Only' – and often for white *men* only.

Oprah's desire to become a **newscaster** and television interviewer was partly inspired by her admiration for Barbara Walters. When Oprah was

'People see me and they see that I am black, that's something that I celebrate. But I don't feel that it's something that I need to wave a banner about, which used to cause me all kinds of problems in college. I was not a dashiki-wearing kind of woman.'

Oprah Winfrey, 1987

growing up, few women of any colour were on television in serious roles. Barbara Walters was the first – and only – television news woman in America in the 1960s. She has a way of gaining people's trust so that she can ask very personal questions and get good answers. 'I thank God for Barbara Walters,' Oprah has said. 'She's a **pioneer** and she paved the way for the rest of us.'

Award-winning journalist Barbara Walters. She was a source of inspiration to Oprah, the young, would-be newcaster.

Role model

Acknowledged worldwide as one of television's most respected interviewers and **journalists**, Barbara Walters became, in 1976, the first woman to co-host a national news programme. Her journalism 'firsts' include an interview with President Fidel Castro of Cuba, and a joint interview with Egypt's President Anwar Sadat and Israel's Prime Minister Menachem Begin (November 1977). She has interviewed every American president since Richard Nixon.

Leaping from Radio to Television

In 1973, Oprah made her vital career move from radio to television. Still in her **sophomore year** of college, she became the first African-American **news anchor** at Nashville's WTVF-TV. She was also the first female co-anchor in the city's history.

Helped by changing times

Before the 1960s, television only hired white men as news readers and talk show hosts. Some people said that the African-Americans and women who were hired in the 1960s were just **tokens**. But in the early 1970s Oprah didn't mind. She felt it gave the opportunity to show people what an African-American woman could do, given the chance. As she put it, 'I was a token, but I was a happy, paid token.' She was also extremely talented. As Chris Clark, from Nashville's WTVF-TV, said of Oprah's audition tape, 'It was unbelievable. You looked at Oprah the first time and you said, "This is right. This will work." It was just one of those things you don't experience very often.'

Challenges in Baltimore

Her next job took her to the eastern coastal city of Baltimore in 1976, as co-anchor of the 6pm television news show with Jerry Turner. Turner wanted a more polished, professional-sounding journalist at his side, but instead he got Oprah, who broke down and cried on the air when she found herself covering one particularly heartbreaking story.

'It was not good for a news reporter to be out covering a fire and crying with a woman who has lost her home. It was very hard for me to all of a sudden become "Ms. Broadcast Journalist" and not feel things.'

Oprah Winfrey, 1994

As Oprah herself put it, 'I was twenty-two years old. I had no business anchoring the news in a major market. Sitting down with the god of local anchormen intimidated me.' On 1 April 1977, she was pulled from the news show. The station attempted to remake her image (which led to her becoming bald after a bad perm). The assistant news director told her that 'her eyes were too wide apart, her nose was too flat and broad, her chin was too big, and her hair was too thick and a complete mess'. But no matter how much they tried to change her image, Oprah's unique style was already in place. She might not have 'looked' like a news anchor-person, but her sincerity, coupled with her clear, midwest accent, enabled her to relate to a wide audience.

LESSONS AND FRIENDSHIP

In the process of working with image makers, Oprah learnt when to listen. She also learnt when to say no to other people's ideas of how she should present herself. She learnt to do news interviews, and how to **network** with people in the business. Baltimore provided an excellent training ground for the star Oprah was about to become.

NETWORKING AND RATINGS

In 1977 Oprah was asked to co-host a local morning talk-interview show, which became *People Are Talking*. Oprah really listened to her audience, which

Oprah in 1986. She proved people wrong when they said 'the talk-show formula was on its way out'.

enabled her to ask better follow-up questions. Soon the Baltimore **ratings** showed her beating nationally broadcast talk-show host Phil Donahue's show – an astonishing feat, given his popularity.

Sherry Burns, producer of *People Are Talking*, took Oprah's natural abilities – and looks – and used them to advantage: 'She's the universal woman… She's a totally approachable, real, warm person. Who she is on camera is exactly what she is off camera… She was and is *the* communicator.' Assistant producer Debra DiMaio said, 'Her stamina was boggling.'

It was Debra DiMaio who helped Oprah land her big break, presenting *AM Chicago*. When DiMaio moved to a Chicago television production job, she showed one of Oprah's *People Are Talking* tapes to station manager Dennis Swanson, who said '... that young woman was sensational. I brought in all my program people, and they agreed. So I called her. When you've looked at as many audition tapes as I have, hers just jumped out of the stack.'

Her best friend, Gayle King Bumpas, was the only one who supported Oprah's move to Chicago. 'Everybody, with the exception of my best friend, told me it wouldn't work. They said I was black, female, and overweight … and the talk-show formula was on its way out.'

Sweet Home Chicago

In January 1984, Oprah jumped into a huge television market when she began to host *AM Chicago*. By 1986, this local TV talk show, now called the Oprah Winfrey Show, was being aired nationwide. More importantly, it was competing well with New York-based *The Phil Donahue Show*. Her popularity surprised even her friends. Oprah explains, 'Chicago is one of the most racially volatile cities anywhere. Our success there shows that race and sex can be **transcended**.'

Not content with being a successful talk-show host, Oprah wanted to be taken seriously as an actress too.

A NIGHT AT THE OSCARS

The show was her day job, but Oprah had 'other fish to fry' after hours. Determined to prove herself as a serious actress, in 1985 she negotiated her role in Steven Spielberg's film of Alice Walker's novel, *The Color Purple*. To be available to film in Hollywood and South Carolina for almost three months, Oprah took time off from her TV show. Guest hosts and re-runs of her old shows aired in her absence, but her fans remained loyal, nevertheless. Her role as Sofia allowed Oprah to express the pain of slavery's heritage. Oprah said Sofia 'represents a legacy of black women and the bridges that I've crossed over to get where I am.' Oprah was nominated for an **Oscar** for Best Supporting Actress.

Oprah as Sofia in the film *The Color Purple*. She is known for her roles as strong, determined women who overcome terrible difficulties.

SIDE PROJECTS GALORE

There seems to be no end to Oprah's projects, large and small. In 1986, with the help of her staff, she formed a Big Sister group for two dozen girls. These girls lived in one of the worst housing projects in Chicago. Oprah met and talked to them herself. 'When we talk about goals, and they say they want Cadillacs, I say, "If you cannot talk correct[ly], if you cannot read or do math, if you become pregnant, if you drop out of school, you will never have a Cadillac, I guarantee it!"' The following year she found time to finish her studies so that she could graduate from Tennessee State University.

Oprah likes to donate to projects, like boys' and girls' clubs, which support and promote African-Americans in the community.

Oprah founded the Angel Network in 1997 to continue the charitable work of Princess Diana and Mother Teresa after their deaths. The Angel Network programmes began with 'Build an Oprah House', in collaboration with the Habitat for Humanity, a worldwide home-building programme founded in 1976 by Millard and Linda Fuller. Oprah's pleas on her shows for support have seen a huge increase in volunteers and donations for this worthy cause. The Angel Network also started 'The World's Largest Piggy Bank', where people give their spare

Oprah performing for race participants in the 1995 Mothers' Day 5K Walk in New York's Central Park.

change to a scholarship fund for poor children. Another project set up by Oprah was the Family for Better Lives Foundation.

Oprah has donated millions of dollars to charity. Her own **alma mater**, Tennessee State University, has received large donations from her. She has given millions to colleges that serve African-American men and women, as well as millions to high schools and boys' and girls' clubs in the Chicago area. Locating her company Harpo in West Chicago has brought prosperity to a run-down part of the city.

'Her public life is very well known. Her private life is very private. I shall only tell you this of her private life: almost any time you read that some anonymous donor has given a great gift to a body of students – black students, white students, Asian, Spanish speaking, Native American, Aleut – when you see "anonymous", whisper to yourself, "Oprah".'

Dr Maya Angelou, introducing Oprah as guest speaker at Salem College in May 2000

FACING PERSONAL PROBLEMS

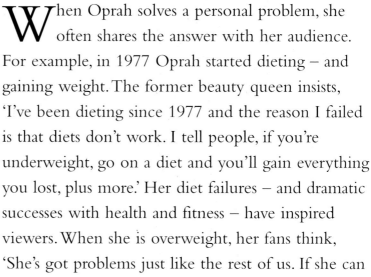

A slender Oprah, shown here in 1996. She has explored issues of weight and fitness on many of her shows.

When Oprah solves a personal problem, she often shares the answer with her audience. For example, in 1977 Oprah started dieting – and gaining weight. The former beauty queen insists, 'I've been dieting since 1977 and the reason I failed is that diets don't work. I tell people, if you're underweight, go on a diet and you'll gain everything you lost, plus more.' Her diet failures – and dramatic successes with health and fitness – have inspired viewers. When she is overweight, her fans think, 'She's got problems just like the rest of us. If she can be successful in life, so can I.' On the other hand, when she exercises, eats right, and looks healthy and slim, her viewers imagine: 'If Oprah *can* solve a personal problem like that, so can I.' Oprah herself once joked: 'If I'm not every woman, I definitely have been every size.'

Oprah now has enough money to pay people to figure out many of her answers. For her diet problem, she hired a chef, Rosie Daley, to help her improve her eating habits. Then she and Rosie co-wrote a

recipe/diet book, *In the Kitchen with Rosie*. It became a best-seller, as did *Make the Connection*, an exercise and fitness book co-written with her fitness trainer Bob Greene. Although Oprah freely admits she loves greasy junk food as much as gourmet meals, her more serious problem was binge eating, especially when she was worried, lonely or depressed. She has explored these issues on many of her shows. Weight and fitness continue to be major concerns for her – and for many of her viewers.

Oprah with her Daytime Emmy Award in 1992. She once tipped the scales at 102 kg (226 lbs).

FACING ABUSE

Sometimes her show forces Oprah to face problems from her childhood. When she was nine, a male relative began to touch her in ways that were inappropriate. She was too young and too afraid to tell her mother then, but she raised the subject of children's sexual abuse on one of her shows. Dramatically and truthfully, she told her story on national television and, in sharing her experience with her audience and viewers, she discovered that she was not alone, which helped her to understand her feelings better.

POVERTY AND THE PAST

Poverty is also a dark side of Oprah's past. Her father owned businesses – a neighbourhood barbershop and a grocery store. This allowed him to give Oprah a middle-class life. Unfortunately, when she lived in Milwaukee, her mother's job only took care of the bare necessities. Now that Oprah is one of the richest women in the world, she has to think carefully about how to help her relatives. She believes she has to balance her generosity with encouragement to self-help, but her mother's side of the family has complained that she doesn't do enough for them.

Now that she is rich, she is also a rich target for lawsuits and has to be careful what statements she makes. After Oprah's 16 April 1996 show about BSE (also called 'Mad Cow Disease'), Texas cattle farmers, worried that her fans would stop eating hamburger meat, tried

Oprah with her defence lawyers during the BSE trial in Texas in January 1998. As one of the most influential women in America, she has to watch what she says.

to sue her for comments she made about beef. She went to Texas to defend herself and, on 26 February 1998, she won in court, and even became friends with some of those farmers.

FINDING TRUE LOVE

Trusting people in personal relationships has been difficult for Oprah. It is hard to trust others when you have had a difficult childhood. It is hard to trust that people truly like you when you are rich and famous.

After years of dating and living alone, Oprah met former athlete and marketing consultant Stedman Graham Jr, in 1986. Talking to *Ebony* magazine, Oprah called Stedman 'an overwhelmingly decent man. He has made me realize a lot of the things that were missing in my life, like the sharing that goes on between two people.' Oprah became engaged to Stedman in 1992. Fans want the thrill of a fancy Oprah-style wedding, but after over fifteen years together, marriage is still too big a step, even for Oprah.

Oprah and fiancé Stedman Graham Jr. Stedman is director of Athletes Against Drugs and president of a public relations firm, the Graham Williams Group.

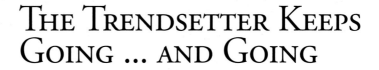

THE TRENDSETTER KEEPS GOING ... AND GOING

*T*he Oprah Winfrey Show still highlights personal problems. But with the increase of copycat talk shows such as *Ricki Lake* and *Montel Williams*, Oprah has moved on. Setting a new trend, she now adds more positive themes. Even when she uses the old, 'problem show', format, Oprah seeks ways to inspire, to help people to help themselves, even while she entertains.

NEW 'SPIRIT'

Now, when she starts with problems, she ends with solutions. One show, for example, interviewed families with 'adult children who mooch and won't leave home' – and who expect their parents to take care of them and pay their bills. They all talked to a **psychologist** on the air. His message was firm: 'Grow up, and take charge of your own life.'

MAKING BOOKS POPULAR AGAIN

Oprah, queen of daytime TV, is now telling her fans to 'turn off the tube' and go and read a book! Or at

Oprah's Book Club

Oprah's choice of books for her club is purely personal, but publishers would love to find ways to influence her or her staff. Since 1996, *Oprah's Book Club* has made millionaires of many of the authors it has featured, and earned **publishers** around $175 million.

*Oprah with Toni Morrison, author of **Song of Solomon**, on Oprah's Book Club in 1996. Originally published in 1977, interest in the book was revived when Oprah selected it on her club.*

least, 'watch my book club show'. Her monthly book club has changed many of her viewers from TV 'couch potatoes' to avid readers and active members of *Oprah's Book Club*.

Each book she highlights on this show rockets onto the *New York Times* best-seller list. A place on this list guarantees success for authors and publishers. It also encourages her viewers to read. In order to be part of her studio audience on the day, you must not only read the suggested book, but you have to write about why you like it. As a result of her book club, many publishers and educators think Oprah is one of America's best forces for literacy.

Professor Oprah's journey

In many ways, Oprah has become one of America's favourite teachers. Not only does she teach values and problem solving on television and on the Internet, but she became a college **professor** as well. Her subject? She taught a graduate-level course in leadership with Stedman at the JL Kellogg Graduate School of Management, Northwestern University. Among the famous guest speakers Oprah brought in were the former US Secretary of State, Henry Kissinger, and (via satellite) the widow of Dr Martin Luther King, Coretta Scott King.

Busy and famous as she is, she still finds time for speaking engagements. In a speech to graduating students at Salem College, an American women's college, in May 2000 she told them: 'I am here because you women will not give up. You wrote me. I got your letters. You emailed. You called. I heard you were going to get in a caravan and come to Chicago. You're relentless. You don't know how to take no for an answer… You are my kind of women.'

These days, Oprah often speaks about her life as a spiritual journey. She says, 'I'm truly blessed. But I also believe that you tend to create your own blessings. You have to prepare yourself so that when opportunity comes, you're ready. I think that the path of our spiritual involvement is the greatest journey we all take. And I think that is part of the reason why I am as successful as I have been, because success wasn't the goal. I wanted to do good work. I wanted to do well in my life.'

In 1999, Oprah was presented with the National Book Foundation's 50th anniversary Gold Medal for all that her book club has done for authors. 'Reading gave me hope. For me it was the open door', she says.

A TYPICAL DAY

Workdays, Oprah wakes up in her two-storey, 24-room Chicago **condominium** between 5 and 6am. From her windows on the 57th floor of the 74-storey Water Tower Place, she has a spectacular view of Lake Michigan, a freshwater lake so big you cannot see across it. She arrives at Harpo Productions between 6.30 and 7am – unless she joins her trainer at 5.30am for a workout at Harpo's fully equipped gym.

The next few hours are spent working with her hairdresser and makeup artist on the wardrobe for the two shows she will tape that day. She tapes over 200 shows a year. While she decides on shoes and earrings and has her makeup done, she talks with her producers about her 'homework': she has studied her guests' biographies, newspaper clippings, and information about the topics of both shows.

Then she tapes the shows. She ends each one by shaking hands with all 500 members of the audience as they leave. Oprah explains: 'It's more memorable than an autograph.' During her break between shows she has

Oprah and Stedman are often on the move between homes. So much travel makes helicopter and jet flights a necessity.

lunch, deals with mail and phone calls, and changes into a new outfit. Her second taping ends at 2pm, when she goes to her mahogany desk and takes on the job of chairman of her multimillion-dollar corporation. Oprah personally decides on all the deals and signs all the cheques.

She can leave as early as 5pm, carrying her homework for the next day's shows. She often stays as late as 10pm. But which home should she go to for dinner? She can take a helicopter to her 160-acre farm in nearby Rolling Prairie, Indiana. It has a TV theatre, a movie screening room, a swimming pool, stables for her three thoroughbred horses, and heated kennels for her dogs, including Solomon, her beloved cocker spaniel.

Or, if she and Stedman feel like skiing, they can get in her private jet, an $18 million 601-3A Challenger, and zip off to her $3 million mountain ski lodge in Telluride, Colorado. If she wants the ocean, she jets to her apartment on Miami's Fisher's Island. Wherever she lands, Oprah says she likes 'coming home, kicking off my downtown clothes, filling that tub with one whole bottle of bubble bath, soaking a good long while, then just putting on my old flowered jammies and a pair of fat socks.' Week nights, she usually reads her homework from 10pm until midnight. Then, as she always has, she kneels to say her prayers.

Unbeatable Oprah

By the age of 46, Oprah was paid at least $70 million a year for *The Oprah Winfrey Show*. This does not mean she will slow down and relax now; far from it. Besides her show, she has a deal to make six *Oprah Winfrey Presents* films for the American Broadcasting Company (ABC).

Kick-starting the millennium

In fact, Oprah has started the new century with a bang. She introduced her own magazine, *O*, in the

Oprah launches *O* magazine in April 2000. She says: 'What I like about *O* is that it is simple and direct, and it is what a lot of my friends call me.'

spring of 2000. It promotes spirituality, community, work and family. She is also challenging her audience to become computer wise.

Oprah teamed up with Geraldine Laybourne (of cable TV's *Nickelodeon*) and the Carsey-Werner-Mandabach production company (which produced TV hits *Roseanne*, and the *Cosby Show*) to launch the cable television and Internet company, *Oxygen*. Designed for women and teenagers, *Oxygen* is expected to eventually reach up to seven million viewers. To promote it, Oprah hosts shows about the Internet. Oprah hopes this will bring women to the World Wide Web in the same way that her Book Club brought them into bookshops.

KNOWING WHAT TO SAY, WHEN

Some wonder if she has some darker secrets she is keeping from the public. She wrote her autobiography, and promoted it at the American Booksellers Association Convention in May 1993. But then she withdrew it from publication because, although all the details of her life were correct in it, she said, 'It didn't have any message. It didn't offer any hope about tomorrow.' She is sure now she made the right choice. She maintains: 'I was still in the heart of the learning curve…. Even in the past year I've learned things about myself that I'm glad I didn't write in an autobiography.'

Building on the Positive

How did Oprah become so successful? She did not come from a perfect family. She was not born with wealth, nor with the kind of looks that often unlock the doors of opportunity for women in television. Instead, Oprah was born with intelligence, talent and an amazing ability to be herself. No matter who the audience, Oprah still appears to be natural and open. Best of all, she can usually say what other people would like to say themselves, if only they dared. Well spoken and warm, she seems to care about people even when she is being blunt with them.

She has been called 'girlfriend to the world', because that is usually how she comes across – to the rich, famous, and ordinary people alike, even to former royalty. After Sarah Ferguson, the Duchess of York, appeared on her show, Oprah told her audience: 'It was like me. I would have been kicked out of the palace, too.'

'Now, when I first started out, I was in the, you know, fat-black-woman box, and nobody could figure out how in the world I had gotten to Chicago being not thin, not blond, not white, nothing that fit the mould of what a talk show host or hostess was…'
Oprah Winfrey, 1997

In some ways, Oprah can do no wrong. When she makes mistakes, her fans like to say: 'She's only human. She's just like the rest of us.' When she is successful, her admirers think: 'Oprah is showing me how I can succeed, too.' Often funny and frequently wise, when Oprah speaks, people listen.

KEY TO SUCCESS

Oprah believes that the key to success is to be prepared for opportunities. She says: 'Doing your best in this moment puts you in the best place for the next moment.'

In October 1994, at the age of 40, Oprah ran in the 42 km (26 miles) Marine Corps Marathon in Washington, DC, finishing in an admirable time.

ON LINE AND IN PRINT

Being prepared to make use of new opportunities has paid off for Oprah. Her own website gives information about *The Show*, *Your Spirit*, and *Living Smart*, and links to other sites such as *Oprah's Book Club*, *Health and Fitness* and her *Online Community* – and there are dozens of other websites about her. Any book she promotes becomes an immediate best-seller. Any diet or exercise programme she tries becomes the latest fitness trend for many. She is chairman of the Harpo Entertainment Group (Harpo, the name of one of the Marx Brothers comedians, is Oprah spelt backwards).

'Focus on this', said an insider at Harpo Entertainment Group. 'She owns the show; she owns the production company; she owns the studio; and now she owns a major part of the distributor.'

A talented actress, in 1998 she starred as Sethe, with Danny Glover, in *Beloved*. In both this latest film and *The Color Purple*, she played African–American women with the courage to overcome terrible difficulties.

The more positive you are about your life, the more positive it will be. The more you complain, the more miserable you will be.'
Oprah Winfrey, 1997

Oprah as Sethe in *Beloved*, with co-star Danny Glover. *Beloved* tells the story of a woman who escaped slavery after the American Civil War.

HELP FROM WITHOUT AND WITHIN

Oprah reminds her public: 'You can't do it all yourself. Don't be afraid to rely on others to help you accomplish your goals.' She praises her staff frequently, often rewarding them with lavish gifts. More than anything, Oprah believes that a positive attitude is the key to success. She also counsels that it is important to listen to your inner self.

THE CHANGING VIEW OF OPRAH WINFREY

Oprah in the midst of her studio audience on *The Oprah Winfrey Show*. Some staff have found it difficult to work with the new, 'positive' *Oprah* show format.

Oprah has been criticized for using serious topics as a form of entertainment. Has she been too quick to use problems to grab ratings? By the mid-90s, many people became tired of reporters 'digging up dirt' about people. Some called this 'feeding frenzy journalism'.

Over the years, guests on her show had sometimes complained that they were misled by Oprah. For example, in 1987 the widows of the astronauts of the exploded Challenger space shuttle thought they had been invited on the show to talk about the Challenger Center. They saw this as a way of turning their tragedy into something positive. Instead, they were asked personal questions about their grief, which upset them. Oprah decided to change. In 1994, she began to focus on

self-improvement issues, pledging to depart from degrading topics. Her ratings took a temporary dip, but she did not give up.

Gradually, her ratings climbed back. She apologized for her past efforts to air the public's dirty laundry for entertainment, saying: 'I've been guilty of doing trash TV and not even thinking it was trash. I don't want to do it any more. But for the past four years we've been leading the way for doing issues that change people's lives...'

While 1994 marked a positive turn for Oprah's show on the air, it was different behind the scenes. That year two of her most trusted employees left the show: one she sacked, the other resigned. The first, Debra DiMaio, who got Oprah her start in Chicago television, had been making life difficult for Oprah's staff. Loyal to her staff, Oprah gave DiMaio several million dollars and asked her to leave.

All Harpo employees have a secrecy pledge in their contract. When her publicist resigned later that same year, complaining about having to continually cover up for 'the disorganized management of Harpo', Oprah refused to give her $200,000 severance pay. At least ten producers left her show over the next two years, which suggests that they found it difficult to work with the new, 'positive' Oprah show format.

BLAZING A TRAIL

Oprah Winfrey is a good example of how a person can make the best use of what they have been given in life. But more than that, she is blazing a trail for women – especially African-American women. She is showing them what they can accomplish when they find that their talents and hard work are matched with equal opportunities in work and education.

'... this woman will be remembered, not in stone wreaths, but by the lives which have grown out of her life, the lives which have been sustained by her life, by the love she gives.'
Dr Maya Angelou, introducing Oprah as guest speaker at Salem College, May 2000

She continues to break new ground. Oprah Winfrey was among the first generation of African-American women to go to **integrated public schools**, and to go to college and university in large numbers. She was one of the first African-American women to be a television **newscaster** – in fact, the very first African-American newscaster in Nashville, Tennessee, where she got her start. Clearly, Oprah had very few **role models** for what women, African-American or white, could achieve. Lacking many role models, she instead became one.

In the world of television, today's success is yesterday's news. Oprah must always keep one step ahead of her competition. What if she should fail?

Many say, having achieved so much, it would be hard to fault Oprah now – and anyway she always views failures as learning opportunities. She counts all her blessings: successes, friends, and even all her difficult lessons in life.

Her journey from poverty and abuse to wealth, fame, and success continues to give hope – and help – to her many fans. She knows who she is, and what she is supposed to do with her life. As she herself explains: 'I'm a truth seeker. That's what I do every day on the show – put out the truth. Some people don't like it, they call it sensational, but I say life is sensational.'

Oprah holding her 1994 BAFTA (British Academy of Film and Television Arts) award for *The Oprah Winfrey Show*, voted best foreign television programme.

Oprah Winfrey – Timeline

1954   (29 January) Oprah Winfrey born in Kosciusko, Mississippi

1960   Leaves grandparents' farm to live with mother in Milwaukee, Wisconsin

1963   Lives with father and stepmother in Nashville for one year

1964   Returns to mother in Milwaukee

1966   Attends Lincoln High School

1968   Attends all-white Nicolet High School in a rich suburb of Milwaukee.

Returns to father and stepmother; enrols in East Nashville High School.

1970   Attends President Nixon's White House Conference on Youth

1971   Represents East High in Outstanding Teenager of America contest. Wins first place in National Forensic League Tournament in Tennessee, goes on to national competition in Palo Alto, California.

1971   Gets her first media job reporting for WVOL radio in Nashville. Begins studies in speech and performing arts at Tennessee State University.

1972   Wins Miss Black Nashville, goes on to win Miss Black Tennessee

1973   Moves to television as Nashville's first African-American anchor at WTVF-TV

1976   Moves to Baltimore for job as co-anchor of 6pm television news.

Asked to co-host local *People Are Talking*, WJZ-TV.

1984   Begins hosting *AM Chicago*, takes it to number one in ratings within one month. Within the year, show is renamed *The Oprah Winfrey Show* and expands to a full hour.

1985   Plays Sofia in Alice Walker's *The Color Purple*. Receives nominations for Golden Globe Award and Academy Award for Best Supporting Actress.

1986 *The Oprah Winfrey Show* becomes number one talk show in America from this year. Plays 'Mrs Thomas' in the movie *Native Son*.

1987 Completes her studies to graduate from Tennessee State University

1988 Receives both the People's Choice Award and the International Radio and Television Society's award as Broadcaster of the Year

1992 Becomes engaged to Stedman Graham Jr

1993 Writes her autobiography, but withdraws it from publication (October).

Forbes magazine lists her as first in the list of 'The 40 Top-Earning Entertainers'; Oprah's worth estimated, at that time, around $240 million.

1994 Pledges to refocus the show on uplifting and meaningful subjects

1996 Receives the George Foster Peabody Individual Achievement Award and the International Radio and Television Society's Gold Medal Award

1998 Named one of the 100 Most Influential People of the 20th Century by *Time* magazine.

Receives National Academy of Television Arts and Sciences' Lifetime Achievement Award.

1999 Presented with the National Book Foundation's 50th anniversary Gold Medal for all that *Oprah's Book Club* has done for authors, books and reading.

Oprah's net worth is estimated at $750 million; paid $70 million a year to do her show.

2000 (April) Launches her interactive cable-TV/Internet website, *Oxygen*, and her monthly magazine, *O*

GLOSSARY

alma mater the school or college you attended

Black Pride a movement begun in the late 1960s by African-Americans to promote pride in their culture

civil rights movement a movement to secure legal civil rights for African-Americans

Coloured a term commonly used, along with Negro, to refer to African-Americans before the Black Pride movement changed the preferred terms to black or African-American

condominium an apartment or home that is owned in co-operation with neighbours

corncob doll a homemade doll made from the dried cob of an ear of maize

curfew a time by which a person must be home or off the streets

dashikis long, loose shirts with bold patterns and colours

Ebony a magazine targeted at African-American readers

Emmy an award given, in the US, to an outstanding television programme or performer

kindergarten the first year of school (at age 5) in the USA, equivalent to Year 1 in the UK

grade schools in the US use this term to mean year: 'first grade' equals the first year after kindergarten

honours student a person who takes a special course of study designed for advanced students

integration bringing the races together, the opposite of segregation

journalist a person who works as a news reporter or editor for a newspaper, magazine, or news programme

mayor the chief elected magistrate of a town or city

networking making connections with people who can be helpful to you

news anchor the chief announcer who introduces a news programme and links other segments of the show

newscaster a person who reports the news on a public broadcast

Oscar a prize awarded annually by the Academy of Motion Picture Arts and Sciences

pioneer a person who blazes a trail for others in a chosen path or profession

production company a company that makes shows for television or movies

professor in the US, a teacher at a university or college

psychologist a person who studies minds and behaviour

public school in America, a school that is required by law to provide a free and appropriate education to all students, regardless of race, religion, or ability

publisher a person or company that produces books and other printed matter

ratings a measure of how many people are watching a show at a given time. Based on surveys of viewers, television stations use ratings to sell advertising time – the more popular the show, the higher the price to advertise during its breaks.

role model someone who inspires others with their skills in a profession or in life

segregate, segregation separate people because of their race, sex or religion

senator a member of the Senate, which is an elected council of US citizens who have the highest legislative function in the US Congress

sheriff the chief law officer in a county in a US state

sophomore year in the US, second year of college

stereotype a conventional, and usually over-simplified, belief or concept

suburb a residential area on the outskirts of a city

token a person hired not necessarily on their own merits but mainly in order to show that a place of business is racially integrated

transcended overcome or rise above limits

INDEX